NEW MILLS

A Century of Change

NEW MILLS LOCAL HISTORY SOCIETY

Preface

The end of a millennium does not come around very often so this seemed to be a good time to look back at a century of momentous change in relation to the life of the Derbyshire town of New Mills. This book of local photographs gives just a glimpse into the life of the town and its people during the twentieth century.

The captions have been written by Olive Bowyer, Barbara Matthews, Derek Brumhead, John Humphreys, and Ron Weston. Thanks are due to the archivist Prof. Roger Bryant for his preparation of photographs and background information. We are grateful to Graham Fletcher for his help with the preparation of photographs.

Acknowledgements

The photographs are drawn largely from the collection held by New Mills Local History Society which is in the care of the Honorary Archivist Prof. R M Bryant. Additional photographs have been loaned by members of the History Society. We are most grateful to all our contributors. Without their generosity books such as this would not be possible. Photographs have been provided by the following people
Archive Holdings Ltd, Mr A Barnard, Mr W Barton, Mr P Beard, Mr A R Belford, Mr H Bowden, Miss O Bowyer, Mrs N Bradbury, Mr H Broadley, Professor R M Bryant, Mr & Mrs B Chatterton, Mr A Clapham, Mrs G Crabtree, Mr J Dean, Derbyshire County Council, Mr J Dixon, Ms A Gadd, Mr R Herdan, High Peak Reporter, Mrs R Hill, Mrs C Rowe, Mrs A Huddlestone, Mr J H Humphreys, Mr B Ibbotson, Mr B S Jeuda, Mrs M Jones, Mr W Kelly, Mrs F Larkum, Miss N Livesley, Ms A Mason, Mr A C Matlow, Mrs B J Matthews, Mr E R Morton, Mr W J Mount, New Mills Town Council, Mr A S Nichols, Mrs Patterson, Mr J G Pogson, Mr K Rangeley, Mrs M Scott, J W Sutherland, Mr J V Symonds, Dr H R Taylor, Mrs Wain, Mr C Wood, Mr & Mrs F Wyatt.

First published 2002 by New Mills Local History Society.

Secretary: Mr J H Humphreys,
17 Cowburn Drive, New Mills, High Peak, Derbyshire, SK22 4EA

© 2002 New Mills Local History Society.

ISBN 1 899109 08 0

edited by Barry Dent, John Humphreys and Ron Weston
designed and produced by Janet Allan,
10 Dale Road, New Mills, High Peak, Derbyshire, SK22 4NW

typeset by Koinonia, Bury
printed by Amadeus Press, Cleckheaton

New Mills Local History Society
homepages.tesco.net/~nmlhs

Introduction

In Britain the twentieth century has brought about change on a scale and at a speed that few people could have foreseen. The skills and strengths of engineering have been all but lost since the Second World War. Coalmining is almost extinct in spite of the existence of huge deposits of coal. The cotton industry has fallen prey to undercutting from abroad. The canals, criss-crossing the country, have become part of the leisure industry. Transport has been transformed by the development of the motor car and huge, long distance lorries. The wood, glue and wires of the early aeroplanes have given way to the sleek, metal jet-planes that can fly faster than sound. Much of this decline has come about in spite of Britain's lead in the development of new inventions and technologies.

New Mills has been influenced by all of these changes and many more but it has not gone into decline like many other towns and cities. The town is more than the visible trappings of an industrial society, its heart is the people who live in the town and the surrounding countryside. A large percentage of the ten thousand population live in family networks that have been around for centuries as can be seen by studying family names. Newcomers began to move into the town, in appreciable numbers, from mid-century onwards. Many commuted to work outside the area but they brought new energy, ideas and skills which contributed to the already thriving life of the town.

Despite the great changes that have taken place during the century the town continues to develop and is very lively in many ways. The last of the mills, Torr Vale, has finally ceased production but some industry remains in the form of Swizzels Matlow Ltd., the largest employer, and a number of small engineering works. The town caters increasingly for visitors and leisure activities with the development of the Sett Valley Trail and other local and long distance footpaths. There is a steady increase in the number of people coming for longer holidays to enjoy the Derbyshire countryside. The opening of the Torrs as a leisure park, following the decline of the mills, has attracted a large number of visitors. The completion of the Millennium Walkway during the last month of the twentieth century has attracted visitors from all over the world.

The book endeavours to record a sample of the life of New Mills over a century of time with the emphasis on the activities of the local people. Who knows what the next century will bring.

In 1898 a peal of six bells was donated to St George's Church by a local councillor, James Hibbert. The bells were cast at Taylor's bell-foundry, Loughborough, and installed in good time to ring in the new century. The bellringing team in 1900 was
[back row] G Hibbert, F Holt, W Marshall, J Ramsey:
[left to right middle row] JH Jackson, S Rutter, AT Beeston [curate];
[front row] W Lowery, J Robinson.
The octave was completed in 1902 with a further donation by Mr Hibbert. Apart from the war years, the church bells have been rung consistently throughout the century.

This group photograph, taken at the wedding of Bertha Ann Hallworth Collier to Fred Holt on 9 January 1899, illustrates the ornate style of dress for a formal occasion. The ladies dressed in black are presumably widows. The group, taken in Hyde Bank Road, is treating the picture-making very seriously.

A gala held on 21 July 1900 in aid of the Indian Famine Fund gave local shopkeepers an opportunity to decorate their premises. Seen here is Broome's butchers, Torr Top Street. The adjacent buildings were situated where the Co-op car park is today.

Calico printing was an important industry in the New Mills district from the early nineteenth century. This artistically staged photograph shows a group of workhands from Birch Vale Printworks about 1900. They seem to be smartly dressed and might well be a department group with the foreman at the right hand end of the front row.

New Mills Silver Band, about 1900. Also known as the New Mills Old Prize Band, it claims to be the oldest band in the country, starting life in 1812. The members had the distinction, in the First World War, of joining the forces as one unit, becoming a military band serving throughout the war, and reverting to a brass band for peace-time purposes at the end of hostilities. This tradition was followed in the Second World War, when the members again enlisted together as a Home Guard Band. The second band in the district was Thornsett Prize Band, with its own headquarters in Thornsett.

Above: Festivities to celebrate the coronation of Edward VII in 1902 draw a large crowd to the Town Hall. On such occasions the procession usually included scholars from the many local Sunday schools and the Friendly Societies marching behind their banners.

Right: Mr James Wharmby and his wife Elizabeth in their car, which is believed to have been the first in New Mills. Mr Wharmby was a grocer and corn-chandler, also responsible for the building of Carlton Villas on Longlands Road.

Albion Road was built during 1834–35 as part of the Thornsett turnpike road system from the Swan Inn at Newtown to Hayfield. At that time it ran across open fields and it was not until the end of the nineteenth century that it became lined with terraced houses and shops linking the new industrial suburb of Newtown with New Mills. At the end of the road can be seen Brunswick Mill, a cotton mill which today is occupied by the sweets firm Swizzels-Matlow. About halfway up the road on the left, on the corner of Wood Street, is the Beehive public house. It was built here in 1902, having been resited from near Brunswick Mill when the Midland Railway line was built and the original pub was demolished. The elegant horse and trap making its way down the centre of the road certainly captures the flavour of the period and the leisurely demeanour of the people standing about and their shadows suggest that this is not a morning of a working day. But is that woman 'donkey stoning' a step on the left?

High Street was once the busiest street in New Mills but has now become a quiet backwater. This view shows shops, long demolished, at the junction of High Street and Stony Brow and opposite the former Wesleyan Chapel. The shop on the left is Eaton, Boot and Shoe Maker. The boy standing in the doorway, next to his mother, is Frank Eaton who later had a shop in Chapel-en-le-Frith.

This photograph shows details of the type of houses once found on High Street, but now long demolished. They stood at the bottom of Stony Brow, at its junction with High Street. The boy nearest, of the group of three sitting on the end of the wall, is Frank Eaton.

This group, of the New Mills Salvation Army, was taken on 12 August 1909 when the Salvation Army founder, General Booth, paid a memorable visit to the town. All the works were closed and the General travelled in a motorcade to the Town Hall where he gave an address. The group is posed in front of the house of Mr Barber, 3 Spring Bank. Mr Barber is on the left of General Booth who is in the centre of the doorway. The band, from the left – Capt. Grace Smith, (3rd) Roger McCormick,(6th) Isaac Rowlands, (7th) Bandmaster Willie Shirt, with euphonium, (10th) — Bennett, (13th) Walter Graham, drummer, (14th) Lt Annie Barr. At the front is another member of the Bennett family.

A procession outside Providence Chapel, Mellor Road about 1906. JW Swindells' horses and lorry are carrying lifeboat boys with souwesters, presumably Sunday school scholars. A group of young girls follow behind. The gentleman wearing the bowler hat is Tom Walker the Sunday School superintendent.

In this early twentieth-century photograph of New Mills Central Station there are many things evocative of the period – the splendid gas lamps, the stone waiting room, the advertisements, the staff maintaining the station, lady passengers in their long coats and hats. In the distance can be seen one of the two tunnels which go under the town. On the right, the station offices and station house built in 1865 which still stand today, a remarkable survival. This line was opened in 1867 and extended to Hayfield in 1868. The smoke comes from Torr Vale Mill.

This is a class of children at New Mills Council School, Spring Bank about 1907. Many of the boys are in smart, white collars and girls wear pinafores to keep their long dresses clean. The single teacher would seem to suggest that this was a class of fifty children. The Headmaster at the time was Mr Crawford.

These men and children, armed with brushes and buckets of whitewash, are about to give the inside of Woodside Mill its annual coat of whitewash. This work could only be carried out when the mill was closed for the 'Wakes Week' holiday. The picture dates from about 1907. The little girl (front right) is Florence Wyatt, aged three. Next to her is Sydney Wyatt and on the far left Ben Garside. Standing behind (from the left) are Thomas Wyatt (Florence's father), Jim Chatterton and Joe Garside, and second from the right is Charley Howard. Who were the men on either side of Charley?

The foundation stone of St James' Sunday School on Spring Bank was laid on 6 April 1910 by Mary Elizabeth Mackie. The building was erected by her family, the Inghams. The church has not had a Sunday School for many years but the building has been used more recently by the Scouts and Guides until it was sold for conversion to a dwelling in Autumn 1998.

This photograph of High Street taken about 1910 reminds us of the variety of elegant Victorian stone buildings that grace our town. The imposing building, centre left, is the Manchester and County Bank, opened in 1862. Beyond it is a range of three shops, with their fine frontages. In a number of cases today such frontages have been restored as part of the town's conservation scheme. The first shop is a stationer–newsagent–tobacconist, H Critchlow, and the billboard says 'Dispatch – Scotch Express wrecked'. Immediately beyond the shops a hanging lamp marks the entrance to the Dog and Partridge pub. On the right is a furnishers, Agent for P & P Dyers Perth.

Standing today in the ruins of Torr Mill (Lowe's), accidentally burnt down on 2 December 1912, visitors often wonder how large a building it had been. This picture shows the building in all its splendour, dominating the confluence of the rivers Goyt and Sett. The River Goyt is in the left foreground flowing towards the weir. On the right is the leat carrying water, drawn from the Goyt at the last bend, to an aqueduct which crossed the Sett. Dr Millward's Memorial Bridge now spans the Sett where the aqueduct once stood and the leat is today a footpath leading to the bridge.

The 1st New Mills, Baden Powell, Scout group on parade during a Camp at Whitsuntide, 1914, at Rhyl, North Wales. The imposing figure on the bass drum is Jack Dean. The Scoutmaster is Mr James Cochran and the Bandmaster is Mr Charles Cooper.

Two contrasting forms of transport of an earlier decade are seen here: a horse-drawn gig and an early motor-car. They are standing outside a former photographic studio which was situated behind Central Garage at a lower level. The sign on the building reads J Derbyshire, Photographer, but printed on the back of the postcard from which this picture is taken are the words M S Ashe, Goyt Studio, New Mills – presumably the successor to J Derbyshire. Standing at the horse's head is Mr S T Stafford and the girls in the gig are (left) his daughter, Fanny, and Betty, possibly another daughter. Albion Road is off the picture to the left.

When this photograph of the Wesleyan Chapel on St George's Road was taken about 1920, the photographer was standing on the New Mill bridge. The chapel was erected in 1810, replacing an earlier chapel on High Street, which still stands although now used by another church. As in other towns and villages of the region, Methodism was very strong in New Mills for over 150 years. But as congregations were reduced, chapels became underused and were sold or demolished. When St George's Chapel, known popularly as 'the old ship', was demolished in 1970, the chapel bell was fortunately saved and can be seen today in New Mills Heritage Centre. The graveyard today, although not in a good condition, has some very interesting grave stones, including that of Paul Mason hanged at Derby in 1813 for theft. On the piece of ground between Hyde Bank Road and St George's Road can be seen a photographer's premises and a monumental mason's yard. Notice the elegant gas lamp.

Young woodworkers at New Mills Secondary School Manual Room, around 1920.

This typical country scene from pre-mechanisation days shows a ploughman working with his team of horses near Aspenshaw. The road winding up the hillside (top left) is Briargrove Road. The original from which this picture was taken was a sepia postcard.

One of the New Mills Co-op coal waggons with horses decorated for a procession about 1930, in a field which is now the area between Hall Street and Meadow Street. Spring Bank School is on the left to the rear and the back of Mount Pleasant Chapel is to the right. The proud declaration on the back end of the waggon is obviously before the days of smog and smokeless zones!

Above: The scene at Salem Cottages and Salem Bridge after the severe flooding of the river Sett in 1930. From a newspaper cutting.

Right: Councillor G A Broome, Chairman of New Mills Council, presenting gifts to old people at a party to mark the Silver Jubilee of King George V and Queen Mary in May 1935.

In March 1935 a new electric pump was installed at Goytside to drive water from Gowhole up to the reservoir at Ballbeard. It replaced the gas engine (able to drive only 6,000 gallons per hour as against the new pump's 12,000) which had been in use since 1908, a turbine having proved unsuccessful and an oil engine inefficient. The electric pump, christened Jean by Councillor J W Cochrane (Chairman of the Water Committee) after his granddaughter (seen on her grandfather's right in the photograph), could raise water to the higher parts of New Mills and was a great asset. Older people remembered queueing for water at wells such as the 'Coffin Spout' on Hague Bar Road, and having to pay a halfpenny a bucket in times of drought – making sure they took the largest bucket they had.

This photograph shows the presentation of trophies to St George's Church of England School at a Sports Day for elementary schools in the New Mills Urban District arranged in July 1935 by Mr A Livesley, President of New Mills Cricket Club. The Senior Trophy, a shield donated some years earlier by Sir Samuel Hill-Wood, for 11–14 years and the Junior Trophy, the Reporter Silver Cup for 8–10 years, were both won by St George's, at that time an 'all-age' school with pupils from 5–14 years of age.

This advertisement appeared in the 'Reporter' in 1935. Note the number of branches the Society then operated, the advantages of membership and the small telephone number – showing the Co-op to have been one of the earliest subscribers in the area.

This healthy looking group (girls aged about 11 years to 13 years) were in Form 1 of St George's Church School about 1931.
Back row from left – Nora Woodhouse, Annie Trotter, Annie Powers, Lilly Lally, ? , (teacher) Miss S C Bradbury, Edna Hall.
Middle row – Betty Stafford, ? Wharmby, Phyllis Crankshaw, Elsie Plummer, Margery Keeling, Lucy Herriott, Emily Hobbs.
Front row – Muriel Gee, Lizzie Marsh, Marjorie Drinkwater, Edna Cooper, Laura Smith, Mary Talbot.

Children playing by Rowarth Brook near Harthill around 1935. In earlier days the swift waters of the brook supplied the water for the reservoirs and water wheels of several small cotton mills.

A pageant in aid of medical charities was the forerunner to the carnival. In 1936 Lily Lomas (right) was crowned Hospital Queen. She is seen here with her retinue which included train bearers Jean Wetters and Janet Ford. Flower strewers were Margaret Lee and Kathleen Taylor, soldiers Jack Parsons, Eric Hibbert, Sydney Rowlands, Harold Froggatt, Phillip Redfern and Alec Redfern. Harold McCormick was the crown bearer and Alfred Coverley the sceptre bearer. The procession included tableaux from eleven local Sunday schools.

A classroom in Hague Bar Primary School about 1948. The girl on the extreme right of the back row is Marion Scott.

The Bate Mill Bowling Club sporting a nice selection of styles of men's headgear of the time, taken about 1937. Third from right, back row, is Joseph Weston.

Aspenshaw Cottages are pictured here about 1938. They stood on Thornsett at its junction with Aspenshaw Road, the area (or more specifically the footpath which provided a short cut between the two roads) being known locally as Doctor's End. The backs of the houses were built into the bank with no doors or windows. A demolition order was placed on them in 1939 as part of a clearance of unfit dwellings, but owing to the war it was not implemented until about 1950. Seen at the top right of the picture is a corner of the Thornsett Congregational Church now a private house.

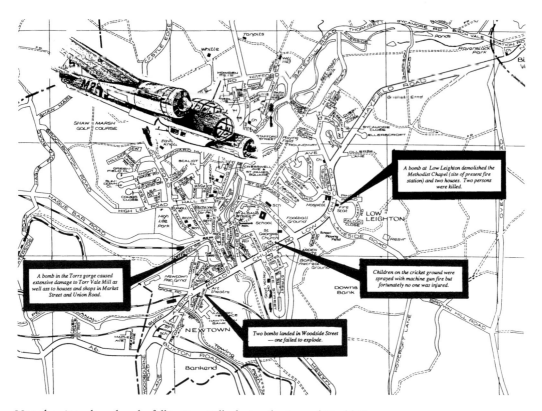

Map showing where bombs fell in New Mills during the Second World War.

The boxes on the map read:

A bomb at Low Leighton demolished the Methodist Chapel (site of present fire station) and two houses. Two persons were killed.

A bomb in the Torrs gorge caused extensive damage to Torr Vale Mill as well ass to houses and shops in Market Street and Union Road.

Children on the cricket ground were sprayed with machine gun fire but fortunately no one was injured.

Two bombs landed in Woodside Street — one failed to explode.

The Book of Remembrance which is on view in the entrance hall of New Mills Town Hall lists the residents of New Mills Urban District who gave their lives during World War Two (1939–45). The War Memorial Committee raised the sum of £2,180 8s 3d (£2,180.41) which provided the Garden of Remembrance, Paddling Pool, Children's playground equipment and seats in High Lea Park as a permanent memorial.

The display shows labels including: CHEMISTRY, ART, CLERICAL WORK, PRINTING, FINISHING, MAKING UP; Simplicity; LOCAL WORKS, STRINES, BIRCH VALE, BINGSWOOD, WATFORD, WOOD; THE CALICO PRINTERS' ASSOCIATION LIMITED

An exhibition of printed fabrics by the Calico Printers' Association in New Mills Town Hall in the 1950s. After this photograph was taken great changes in the local industry took place in the next few years. The CPA consortium was formed in 1899 and most of the printworks in north-west England, including local ones, became members. However, reorganisation of the cotton industry, competition from cheap imports and artificial fabrics resulted in wholesale closures in the 1960s.

During the 1940s canal transport was motorized, though the horse being led along the towpath (centre left) may indicate the presence of a horse-drawn boat just out of sight. Coal was still being taken to the mills by canal during and just after World War Two. Note the 'butty' (a boat with no engine) which was towed by the leading boat, thus increasing the load which could be carried. The closure of the Whaley Bridge section of the Cromford & High Peak Railway in 1952 sounded the death knell of commercial traffic on the Upper Peak Forest Canal.

This horse-drawn narrowboat passing through Bridge 21, Plucks Bridge (Strines), on its way up to New Mills is typical of many which regularly plied the Upper Peak Forest Canal for some 150 years up to the decade prior to World War Two, though the volume of traffic declined after the closure of the Peak Forest Tramway by an Act of Parliament in 1925 and the consequent closure of Bugsworth Basin. Goods, especially coal, were still taken to and from the group of textile mills at Newtown, which indeed owed its existence and continuing prosperity to the transport facilities provided by the canal.

On 21 April 1951 a steam train approaches the fine array of signals in front of the twin tunnels under the town. The signals indicate that the train is cleared to enter the left-hand tunnel on its way to Hayfield. The tunnel on the right led to Sheffield and Derby, the line dividing at Chinley. This tunnel is still open (for trains to Sheffield only), the line to Hayfield having been closed in 1970. On the right is the huge retaining wall above the river Goyt. The Millennium Walkway is built along the base of this wall.

This superb photograph was taken about 1948 when retiring employees of Birch Vale Printworks were each presented with an identical clock. At this time, before early retirement was even heard of, the men would have been 65 years old and the women 60. After the works was extended in the 1850s the terrace of cottages in the background was built.

New Mills Secondary School was originally located (along with the Elementary School) in the school buildings on Spring Bank. It was a significant event, therefore, in the educational history of New Mills when a new school building was erected on open fields in 1914. In the 1920s it became New Mills Grammar School and remained as such until comprehensive education was introduced in the 1960s. Today the former playing fields around the school are covered with other buildings. The photograph shows Dale Road under construction about 1920. Hyde Bank Road was built in 1835 as part of the Thornsett turnpike, a road leading to New Mill Bridge over the river Sett. The terraced stone houses were not built until the first decade of this century, when a lot of house building took place in New Mills. Notice the horse-drawn milk float. The ground on the right with the construction materials is now the site of the Kingdom Hall, the meeting place of the Jehovah Witnesses.

A children's party in the Town Hall to mark the coronation of Elizabeth II in 1953. Throughout the century, tea parties were a traditional way of celebrating such national events.

St Luke's Church, Birch Vale about 1955 with the Sycamore behind. The 'tin tabernacle' was erected around 1903 and for many years was a well attended church. A Sunday school was added later. In 1973 a fire badly damaged the vestry and the church was closed. By this time the congregation had dwindled down to a faithful few. In February the following year the church re-opened for one service before the doors were closed for the last time. The building was later demolished.

In the days of commercial canal traffic these stables were part of the complex of the Peak Forest Canal Company's wharf and warehouse, the site of which is now occupied by New Mills Marina. In the interests of speed and efficiency horses pulled boats for a limited distance only; tired horses were then rested and later pulled another boat (or the same one on its return journey) back to its starting point. New Mills was such a changing place; the stables, which stand to the south-east of the warehouse, well back from the canal, provided shelter for the horses during their rest period. The two storey building with the circular opening was the hayloft, where fodder for the horses was stored. Unfortunately this part of the building became unsafe and was demolished some years ago. The stables are thought to date from about 1830.

The Sett valley was an important sub-centre in north-west England for the so-called finishing trades, namely the bleaching, dyeing and printing of cotton cloth. Huge works grew up on the river floodplain for the industry required many acres of land for its extensive buildings and huge reservoirs. This photograph, taken in the late 1960s, of Birch Vale Printworks illustrates all this very well. The works were demolished in the 1960s, and the site is now occupied by the modern buildings of a firm producing polymers. The single line railway, which ran past the works, joined New Mills and Hayfield. It was closed in 1970 and now forms the Sett Valley Trail, a route for walkers, cyclists, and horse riders. The conspicuous road running up onto the moor is Moorland Road. The large house in the trees is Moorland House, built in the late nineteenth century by the Hall family, who managed the local coal mines.

The junction of Market Street and Union Road about 1970 showing The Railway (now The Peaks), Alsop & Clayton decorators and The Crescent Inn and Foy's greengrocery stall, hence the local name of Foy's corner for the area. This business later moved to a shop in Market Street and a small garden was constructed where it once stood.

Market Street, about 1970. New Mills Co-operative Society had been trading in the town since the 1860s. In the 1970s the several shops that the Society owned passed into the hands of other traders.

This unusual picture dating from the 1960s shows elephants (walking in the time-honoured manner, each holding with its trunk the tail of the elephant in front!) turning the corner by Burfoots' Newsagents Shop from Albion Road to Union Road. They belonged to the well-known Gandy's Circus which visited Newtown Football Field periodically. The parade through the town was a publicity stunt. One of the posters on the side wall of the shop advertised the circus, and the shopkeeper received a free ticket for displaying it. Hurst Lea House, the large building behind the shop, formerly the doctors' surgery and now the Police Station, was until 1963 the Liberal Hall. Note the old electric lamp (a converted gas lamp) and the tall concrete standard about to replace it. The guard rails round the corner of the footpath were removed when the traffic lights and pedestrian crossing were installed in the mid-1970s.

The new Fire Station at Low Leighton, built on the site of the Methodist Church demolished by an air-raid on 3 July 1942, replaced the out-dated and inadequate building on Hague Bar Road (now a Council Depot). It commenced operation in August 1969, though not by then officially opened. The streamlined Dennis appliance featured in the photograph, at that time five years old, was one of two stationed at New Mills, with the promise of a third to come. The new station was one of the most modern in the country. It took 18 months to build and the package included 12 firemen's houses. So sophisticated was the system of communications that on pressing a button in Buxton Fire Station the siren at New Mills sounded, the doors opened and the lights were switched on ready for the departure of the appliance, and the doors closed 30 seconds after it had passed through them. The station provided training and recreational facilities, lecture room, kitchen and dining room, showers and drying room. The high tower provided scope for training in rescue work, having a variety of different window-frames built into the front. It was also used for drying hoses, and the room at the base was equipped for servicing breathing apparatus. A 30 foot well in the yard was used by all Buxton Division for testing pumps. Who was the fireman about to drive the appliance?

Up to the early 1960s, there were important railway good stations at Church Road and Newtown, which distributed coal and other industrial supplies around the town. At Newtown there was a goods transfer shed and substantial railway sidings, as this photograph shows. One of the lines ran underneath the signal box, which must have been a smoky place! Today, this is all waste ground, although the warehouse still stands and is used by a local firm. In the background are Albion Mill and Brunswick Mill, former cotton mills built on the banks of the Peak Forest Canal. The conspicuous long low building in front of the mills is a rope walk.

Many local people, young and old, were skilled workers in various trades in the printworks, as artists, tracers, engravers, and pantagraph operators. This photograph, taken in the late 1960s, shows the painstaking work involved in preparing patterns for fabrics at Watford Bridge Printworks. As a result of this work, firms built up a series of pattern books, which, except for a few cases, were unfortunately not saved when the firms closed. Some pattern books, however, donated by former employees of local printworks, can be seen on display at New Mills Heritage Centre.

J J Hadfield's Garrison Works was situated in the Sett valley between Thornsett and Birch Vale. This photograph, taken about 1961, shows the final inspection of bleached fabrics prior to despatch. Stains were removed and the fabrics then ironed.

The demolition of the chimney at Watford Bridge Printworks at 12.30 pm on 7 May 1966, marking the end of an era which had started in 1804 when fourteen acres of land were first leased for a printworks. The works were greatly expanded in the late nineteenth century and like several other local printworks, these works became part of the huge consortium known as the Calico Printers Association. But the 1960s marked the closure of all the local printworks such as those at Birch Vale and Hayfield, and the bleachworks at Thornsett. Today very little remains of this once great industry which employed hundreds of skilled local people. Many still live in the town, and the Heritage Centre has benefitted from gifts of engraving tools, pattern books, recipe books, and other material of great historic interest.

New Mills Swimming Pool Association revived the carnival in 1974 after an absence of 27 years. The purpose was to raise funds for a swimming pool for the town. Anne Barrow, an examiner at Strines Printworks, was crowned the first carnival queen on 15 June. Her attendants were Alison Payne and Joan Potts.

These youngsters, from the Peak Road area, dressed to depict characters from nursery rhymes, are on one of the many floats in the 1974 New Mills Carnival procession. They were doing their bit to raise money for a much needed swimming pool.

The weather on the first carnival day in 1974 was glorious. Here a group of local residents in festive mood are enjoying both the sunshine and the procession as it passes along Watford Bridge Road.

After having been closed for twenty-five years, a plan to reclaim and re-open the derelict land around the gorge in the Torrs was instigated by New Mills Civic Amenities Society. The work was carried out by New Mills Urban District Council at a cost of £50,000, the Department of the Environment granting 75% of this amount. The area was landscaped, paths laid and seats provided. Graham Ashworth, Professor of Environmental Studies at Salford University, opened The Torrs on 21 September 1974.

The Co-op shops, numbers 21–27 Market Street, are shown here at the commencement of demolition in 1981. The Co-op branch, which had been in New Mills for 121 years, had closed down following a meeting of members in February 1973 when they voted to join the Norwest Co-op, a larger organisation. The shops were cleared as part of the preparation for building a new Norwest Co-op store in Torr Top Street. The area shown has now become the Promenade, a useful meeting place for local groups.

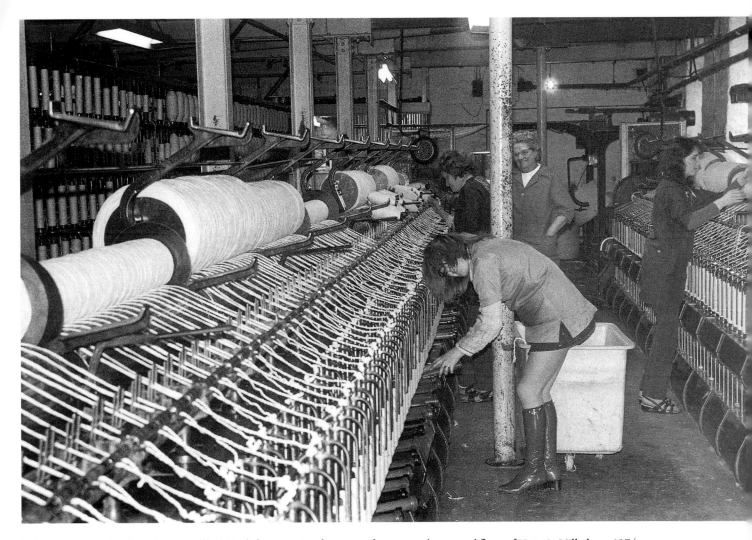

This scene shows 'doffing' (taking off bobbins) from a pair of spinning frames on the ground floor of Victoria Mill about 1974. Victoria Mill was the last of the cotton spinning mills in New Mills, closing down in 1985. It was destroyed by fire in 1986. The workers at the back are Mrs Pritchard, Mrs Bradbury and June Woodward but who is the young lady, bending, showing off the fashion wear of 1974?

During the 1980s a Play Scheme was organised by volunteers for a week of the school summer holidays. It was held in High Lea Park and provided a variety of activities, covering various sports and hobbies. This picture of participating children was taken near High Lea Hall in August 1984.

The carnival continued to be the main fundraising event for the Swimming Pool Association into the 1980s. Here regulars of the Crescent and the Young Wives Group have joined together to form a morris dancing troupe of Mrs Mops. The leader is Diane Trueman followed by [left to right] Margaret Beddows, Chris Sullivan and Barbara Coffey. The mini mops are Louise Coffey and Amanda Trueman.

The Millward Memorial Bridge was erected in Spring 1984 to mark the centenary of the opening of Union Road High Level Bridge in 1884. The huge oak beams, 41½ feet long and weighing 1¼ tons, were lowered over Church Road Bridge, due to the inaccessibility of the site to large vehicular traffic. The bridge is named after Dr Millward, who pioneered the opening of the Torrs to public access and establishing the Riverside Park in the early 1970s. The bridge provides a link between the Torrs and Sett Valley Trail and Goytside, and eventually became part of the Goyt Way and later of the Midshires Way.

On 7 June 1984, to celebrate the centenary of the opening of Union Road Bridge, a procession of townspeople dressed in Victorian costume walked from the Town Hall to Union Road where Councillor Gordon Allen carried out a re-enactment of the opening of the stone built viaduct. Teacher Des Hoskisson is seen here leading children from Thornsett Primary School.

Above: The Heritage Centre was opened officially on 8 April 1989 when a good crowd assembled to hear Brian Redhead give one of his usual stimulating addresses. The Centre had been opened to the public since the previous July. As so often happens on such occasions in the town, New Mills Band was present and so was the New Mills steam roller bought by New Mills Urban District Council in 1924 for £776 and sold in the 1960s. Since then it has remained in private hands locally, one of the very few steam rollers to remain working in its home area.

Right: Brian Redhead meets Ivy Eddleston, Olive Bowyer, and Nora Lloyd, all volunteer assistants, in the Heritage Centre shop.

In 1988 feelings in the town reached fever pitch when the Department of Transport announced its plan to construct the proposed A6 Disley/High Lane bypass, The Brown Route, along the valley of the Goyt between Hague Bar and Furness Vale. On Sunday 21 February 1988 a ribbon of 2,000 people walked the route to show their opposition to the construction of the road.

The unveiling of the plaque on the former New Mills Police Station on Hall Street commemorating the Kinder Mass Trespass in 1932, which ultimately led to the granting of public access to open country on Kinder Scout. The ceremony was performed by Benny Rothman, who as a young man played a prominent part in the Trespass and was imprisoned in the cells of this building. Here he is seen holding a photograph of the plaque which was presented to him by Councillor Martin Doughty on behalf of Derbyshire County Council.

There was great excitement in the town when HRH The Princess of Wales arrived at Swizzels Matlow's New Mills sweet factory on 14 June 1990. The factory yard was packed with employees past and present, and the tranquillity of the staff car park was shattered by 300 local schoolchildren who waited excitedly to catch a glimpse of the Princess.

The Princess was taken on a tour of the factory, which is the town's largest employer, by the joint managing directors Trevor Matlow and Michael Dee.

Swizzels Matlow pensioners enjoyed a grandstand view of the Princess as she arrived at the factory. Three had worked in the original London factory, which was founded in 1928. During the Second World War blitz, the factory, together with some of the female employees, were moved to New Mills. When the War ended, they decided not to return to London, and remained in the town working for the company

In the centre of this aerial photograph taken in the early 1990s is a small building with a chimney. Built about 1837, this building was Yates' brass works. Although the site is now occupied by sheltered housing, the chimney being in the town's conservation area was thankfully preserved, and today is the oldest surviving chimney in the town. On the left is Torr Top car park, where until the late 1950s there were terraces of houses similar to those in the bottom centre of the picture. When Market Street, on the right, was built in the first years of the nineteenth century it ran across open fields. As the cotton industry got under way and the town grew, it soon became lined with houses and shops. The bus station has had a varied history, being New Mills first outdoor market in the 1920s, and later a car park.

Above: The Reverend Jenny Morten, curate at St George's Parish Church from 1990 to 1994, greeting parishioners at St. James's Church. During her time at New Mills, Jenny became one of the first women priests to be ordained in the Derby Diocese.

Right: Well-known local shopkeeper Bill Barton with son John. The Barton family have been in business in Market Street for nearly thirty years and represent the need for the continuity of local family businesses in small towns.

Left: New Mills School's production of the musical *Oliver* was performed at the Art Theatre in 1980. The part of Oliver was played by Michael Pitcher (seated).

Below: In November 1994 New Mills Operatic and Dramatic Society staged one of its most ambitious projects. The musical *Barnum* was a colourful spectacular showing all forms of circus entertainment from tightrope walking to trapeze acrobatics.

March 1949 saw J B Priestley's play *When We were Married* performed by members of New Mills Amateur Operatic and Dramatic Society at the Town Hall. The principal players, from a cast of 14, included (left to right) C F Astley-Jordan, Edmond Haughton, Eric Crosland, Margaret Nesbit, Betty Schofield and Sheila Willford.

Below left: The former cinema in Union Road, always known as 'The Cinema', became 'The Star Bingo and Social Club'. Cinema-going went into a serious decline in the 1960s with the growing popularity of television. The picture was taken when the building was awaiting demolition early in 1988. The Arts Theatre is also a former cinema.

Below right: The demolition team get to work on the old cinema and soon it is no more. Its place is taken by 'Stax' a new leisure and entertainment centre.

The children of St George's Church of England Primary School celebrated their school's 150th anniversary in October 1996. To prepare for the event the children studied the Victorians and during a week of celebrations were allowed to wear victorian costume at school. The school moved to its present site in 1864. Originally it was situated in the vicinity of the Sett Valley Trail on land donated by William H F Cavendish.

Headteacher Mr Phil Thomas (then acting head at St George's) is holding a journal containing the minutes of meetings and correspondence dating from 1845 about the setting up of the original school. The building was financied by public subscription and a list of subscribers included William Egerton of Tatton Park, Strines Printworks. HM The Dowager Queen Adelaide (widow of George IV) contributed £10.

The Heritage Centre provides a base with its education room and educational officer, Jane Featherstone, for local children who carry out investigations to develop their knowledge and understanding of New Mills. Hundreds of children come every year from nearby towns and cities to explore themes as required by the national curriculum. They consider the contrast between a small Derbyshire town and their much larger towns and cities. This picture shows a group of primary age children studying the ruins of the cruck barn at Mousley Bottom, which is thought to be the oldest building in New Mills.

This street scene shows the upper end of Market Street at its junction with High Street. There is not much traffic, allowing a man to walk down the middle of the street and a horse and cart to block most of Market Street but then this was about 1900! Note the ladies drawing water from the well on the pavement.

The passage of 100 years has changed the junction of Market Street and High Street considerably. Pedestrians cross at their peril, traffic calming measures have been introduced together with a 20mph speed limit and we have our own 'friendly' traffic warden, Judith Skinner (standing on the corner of High Street).

As part of a nation-wide project that every church bell in the country should be rung at the millennium the team of bell ringers at St George's church were ready to ring in the year 2000 [left-to-right: back row] Paul Beard (Tower Captain), Lauren Roebuck, Neil Radford, Margaret Edge, Anne Hopley, Brenda Wise, Margaret Wood [front row] Rachel Murdoch, Reg Radford, Rita Hill, Elaine Radford, Christine Murdoch.

Publications of New Mills Local History Society

New Mills History Notes (A5 format)

1 New Mills in the 1820s: Part I
  (extracts from Stockport Advertiser)
2 New Mills in the 1820s: Part 2
  (extracts from Stockport Advertiser)
3 Whitle Enclosure
4 The mills of New Mills
5 New Mills 1830-35 (extracts from Stockport Advertiser)
6 Railways of New Mills and district
7 Turnpike roads and riots
8 The lost mills of Rowarth
9 The New Mills Tithe Award (central area) – (including map)
10 Deeds of New Mills and district
11 The Peak Forest Canal: Upper level towpath guide
12 A history of Providence Congregational (Independent) Church, New Mills
13 Memories of Strines
14 The lost chapel of Rowarth
15 The coal mines of New Mills
16 Bowden Middlecale - the occupants of the land 1778-1811
  (From Land Tax Assessments)
17 More deeds of New Mills and district
18 New Mills 1835-39 (extracts from Stockport Advertiser)
19 Three local history walks
20 New Mills Co-operative Society 1860-90
21 The New Mill and some other corn mills of the High Peak
22 The New Mills Air Raid: Friday 3 July 1942
23 The Peak Forest Canal. Lower Level Towpath Guide
24 The living past: New Mills people in late Tudor and early Stuart times (from probate documents)
25 The Downes family, husbandmen in the New Mylne 1571-1697 (from probate documents)
26 A Lifetime at Strines Printworks
27 The Hayfield Union Workhouse
28 Men of Property: The Bowers and the Newtons

Probate Transcription Series

Wills and Inventories of New Mills People (general title)
Book One   1540-1571
Book Two   1571-1582
Book Three   1586-1607

Occasional Publications (A4 and A5 format)

OP 1   Gravestone inscriptions: St George's Road Methodist Cemetery
OP 2   New Mills and district: a look back (old photographs)
OP 3   The Peak Forest Canal: its construction and later development
OP 4   Church of the Annunciation St Mary's Catholic Church, New Mills, Graveyard records
OP 5   Ollersett in 1841: land and people
OP 6   New Mills in 1851 and 1881 as seen through the census returns (Comparative analysis of data using a computer)
OP 7   The mills of New Mills (Revised and greatly expanded edition of New Mills History Notes No 4)
OP 8   The enclosure of Thornsett
OP 9   Thornsett in 1841: land and people
OP 10 New Mills: a look back at its Industrial Heritage
OP 11 Where Two or Three are Gathered Together: A History of St Paul's Church Strines

For further details regarding availability or orders please contact Ron Weston, Editor, New Mills Local History Society, 'The Thorns', Laneside Road, New Mills, High Peak, Derbyshire, SK22 4LU. Tel. 01663 744838

Publications of New Mills Heritage Centre

The Torrs Riverside Park Bridges Trail
The Torrs Industrial Trail
Waterside Circular Walk, (New Mills-Hague Bar)
The Torrs and Peak Forest Canal: History Trail
A short history of New Mills
Strines History Walk
New Mills 1894-1994
Urban District Council Surveyor, 1946-74

For details or orders please contact the Administrator, New Mills Heritage Centre, Rock Mill Lane, New Mills, High Peak, Derbyshire, SK22 3BN.

New Mills Local History

New Mills Local History Society was formed in 1983. With the help of the general public, it has built up a large collection of books, documents, photographs, and miscellaneous items relating to the history of the district. These can be consulted by arrangement. The Society presents a programme of evening lectures in the autumn and spring, excursions in the summer, and from time to time holds exhibitions on various aspects of local history. It has also been prominent in publishing a number of publications on the history of New Mills and district, most of which are still in print. In association with Derbyshire Library services, it has contributed to the cost of a microfilm and microfiche reader in New Mills Library, and has provided various microfilms for use by the general public, including the popular IGI genealogical index. In 1988, it was closely involved with the establishment of New Mills Heritage Centre, owned and run by New Mills Town Council, and is represented on the management committee. Many of the society's members work for the centre in a voluntary capacity. Enquiries about the society may be made at New Mills Library or at New Mills Heritage Centre.

On the web:
New Mills Local History Society   www.homepages.tesco.net/~nmlhs
New Mills Heritage Centre   www.newmills.org.uk